YOU ARE
ALWAYS CIRCLING

YOU ARE
ALWAYS CIRCLING

Poetry

Audrey Tanner

Kinstu Books

Revised edition 2026

Cover design by Audrey Tanner using elements from Canva.com. Elements attributions: Photo by Audrey Tanner; @ Ksuview via Canva.com; @ sofiastd via Canva.com.

Published by Kinstu Books in the USA

Hardcover ISBN: 979-8-9875531-3-8
Paperback ISBN: 979-8-9875531-4-5
Ebook ISBN: 979-8-9875531-5-2

For Jared, ever circling.

With highest regard for the inherent human longing for spiritual transformation, and for the many forms of practice and tradition that may lead one to Self.

TABLE OF CONTENTS

BREATH WANTS 1

THIS IS THE DANCE 9

WHY MUST YOU WAIT 19

MARICHAYE (DAWN) 25

MARICHAYE (DUSK) 31

HERE 37

CHRYSALIS 45

YOU ARE ALWAYS CIRCLING 53

BREATH IN THE SHAPE OF A BEE 65

WATER BLESSING 75

WALK AMONG TREES 85

BREATH INHALES 93

STEP INTO A FOREST 99

DEER CROSSING A RIVER 105

SKY AS AN OCEAN 111

SO BELOVED, BELOW 117

TREE-SOUL 129

TIGER LILY 137

ALWAYS 147

BREATH WANTS

In love with living, breath
wants to rush when it sees

the full moon shining through
slivers of winter trees,

branches bare and bowing
in frigid wind,

wind winding its way around
tree trunks and through

the seams of your jacket,
cells of your skin.

In love with standing,
breath wants to know

a beginning and ending
of the seamless night blanket,

depth of space, coldness
collapsing into black holes;

the soul ever wandering,
reborn into pitch

of stars commencing,
light expanding.

In love with breathing,
breath wants to wait

for a symphony of stars
that light the blue-dark night,

stars with circling planets,
worlds with oceans frozen,

oceans of breath breathing
while the wind whips through

the shell of your jacket,
shell of your soul.

In love with being, breath
wants inhale and exhale

of night turning to morning,
a forecast of snow;

clouds commencing,
snowfall a complete

circle of being, snow,
melt, evaporation, cloud, snow;

soft flakes falling to ground,
soft into the heart.

In love with heart beating,
breath wants to feel

snowflakes falling, soft
or sharp, light or crystalline

heavy, sky-flowers falling
into icy contagion to

gather snow all
around you, whispering

your secrets of being,
secrets of soul.

THIS IS THE DANCE

This is a dance,
the sun and you
spinning snow
into flowers.

Snow melts,
your root-heart
melts. Sometimes
just as you

are ready to open
there is late snow.
Your roots will endure
this, sun will shine again.

Before winter came
you hid your head.
You planted yourself
in dirt as fall heart-

bulbs, crocus, daffodil.
Sun retreats, spinning
dances into weather
that is too cold for you.

In winter you endure
the frozen ground;
beneath snow you long
to dance in warmth again.

You lean into frozenness
because it is needed.
This is how you understand
a cycle of seasons.

A time to hide, a time
to grow. This is the cycle
of sun and you.
Sun spins earth away

only so that it may
return to you
after the March equinox,
once snow stops falling.

Winter recedes
with a whirl of dance;
snow becomes rain, seasons.
The sun's love warms

again. All that is asked
of you is to open your
crocus and daffodil
wherever you may

have been planted.
These are but
soft-scented tokens
to begin.

Through winter
your heart-bulbs wait
for proof that you
can dance again. In spring

the sun begins to spin
you into flowers. Snow melt
anoints you. Snow
becoming icy water is

the sun's act of love.
This dance
is the only dance: heart-thaw,
renewal, life becoming.

Sun waits while you
look for signs
of your desire
to burst into being.

Patience is required.
You may push up
fragile stalks or frost
may have you fail.

This is a dance,
a test of faith.
A root-heart frozen
or burgeoning rebirth.

Spring comes,
your root-heart
surfaces into love.
You dance

in the flowers
you have become,
circling with
sunshine.

This is the dance,
to take the waiting
heart-bulbs into
blossom after snow.

WHY MUST YOU WAIT

Why must you wait
for flowers to
be named in order
to become?

It is already time
to open your scent
of bluets and pansies,
violets and chickweed.

You are in the rain
and sun. In the dirt
you may propagate
yourself into

tickseed and tulip,
rue anemone.

Without sunlight
you are still potential.
In drought you are
a seed waiting.

Here at the edge
of garden or wild in forest,
wherever you have planted
yourself, you will find rain.

You will become tall
and open. In the south
light you will receive
yourself as soft

things growing. Purple
vinca, soft froth of azalea.

Do not wait
for flowers to be named
in order to become
yourself. Your roots

are always there.
You are always
around yourself
as you open, your own

community of flowers.
Here, this is always true;
now, as spring rain
offers you space

to become dandelion
and celandine, cherry blossom.

MARICHAYE (DAWN)

Dawn always
pours silver melt

into day;
night stirs into silver as

you awake knowing
the meaning

of daylight is soft

smelted glaze. Sunrise

is a treasure,
a moment of being,

Om Marichaye
Namaha.

Melt into this
and you become

burnished, smooth
treasure, a chest

of precious metal
that has been

hidden by night.

Om Marichaye

Namaha:
Melt and you

are dawn, daylight
becoming.

There in daybreak
as night silvers

into dawn, you
know who you are,

light of sun
light of heart warming

into being,

inter-being, soft smelt

of night, day,
radiant essence:

Om Marichaye
Namaha.

MARICHAYE (DUSK)

You hold
both halves

of mystery,
light, dark. Unfolding

into this you become
mantra,

Om Marichaye,

cloth of day and night.

Weave yourself
into sky becoming

soft garment of self,
dusk of soul.

Twilling time
from day, night,

there is no
separation into

velvet dark becoming.
You have always

known night

is beauty, day

a friend. Weave
yourself into soft

mantra from the heart:
Om Marichaye, Om.

Soft threads
of silver converging

from day, night.
You already

know you are
threads of tapestry,

inseparable,

intertwined into

being. Weave
yourself into deep

night becoming. Om
Marichaye Namaha.

HERE

You go in, in
to the place where
wild things dwell. Here
you begin to remember
the essence of love.

Here in the woods
with yellow wildflowers
that grow on a hillside
sloped down to a lake,
you forget who you are,
who you may become.

Here you can wash
your feet in a stream
while birds sing.
Here you wash yourself
in nature's symphony

of red-crested
woodpecker, cardinal
and crow. Blue jay
and hawk, other birds, bird-
songs whose music is
mysterious, names forgotten.

You can only
speak for yourself.
You can only say your name
is Audrey.
Your past is your past,

your karmas inborn with you.
Here, karmas follow you like
gnats or with the scent
of wildflower bloom.
Karmas flow to you
as a river.

Here, there may be catbirds,
these birds, other birds
whose names escape memory.
In spring, after daffodils,
goldfinches appear,

soft karmas that come
into green branches.
Here, by a stream that flows
into a river, peace comes,
softly inside, alongside
all wild things.

You go down, down
to the water's edge.
Here a crow
calls to you from
a high branch, a blessing

or warning. There is
a name for you
that crows call.
Here memory renews
a rough translation,
a song of love.

CHRYSALIS

Everything requires
waiting. Your cater-
pillar body waits
to become pupa.
Your pupa body waits
to grow wings.
Wings wait

to extend in warm air
that smells
of jasmine. Your
heart waits until
you come out
of chrysalis, unfolding
as a treasure.

Open your chrysalis
purse. Here you will
find that what lays
at the bottom
has always been
the price of becoming.
You can emerge

with whatever
wings are needed.
Your soft cater-
pillar body, pupa,
have always been
only soft change,
malleable coinage.

You are first
one wing then
the other, complete.
You emerge from your
shadowy purse of
chrysalis and
dip yourself into

golden sunlight.
In this act
you can become
as soft as you have
always been, a butterfly
revealing treasure,
unfolding love.

Chrysalis requires
patience. Emerging into
sunlight is an
act of love.
Emerging as self,
you can become grace
in a bright gem ascent,

descent. Birthing self
requires chrysalis
to have been spun
around your heart,
fragile and enough
for your butterfly
self to become.

You have always had
hues in your soul
that have been
unspoken. Red,
bronze, soft gems
in the substance
of fragility.

When you emerge
from chrysalis
you can finally unfold
your tips of azure
and gold. Wings
unbound, you can
finally extend, fly.

YOU ARE ALWAYS CIRCLING

Butterflies will come,

delighting in the deep
floral of you. Bees

will circle forever
in the essence of you.

Bees circle knowing
only of your flowering-ness.

Allow yourself
into your own garden

in order to see
the subtle shape of your

rose-sweet prana.

You open and wait

knowing you will come
to self as magnificent

insects come, always circling.
In sunshine, bees delight

in prana that buzzes
around your heart.

Butterflies know
you are confection

of daffodil and primrose,
primal sustenance,

deep ambrosia.

The shape of flowers,

the body, is not all
that you are.

In the butterfly's touch
transmutation begins.

You may become
bee or flower, scent

of jasmine, fragile wings.
Stigma and stamen

of self, pollen
and nectar; prana

of love always circling.

Butterflies and bees

have the same instincts
of heart. Which

you may become
does not matter

as much as knowing
that the gentle touch

of wings is love.
Either way, you may open

your delicate wings
to sunshine and drink

the blooming prana of self.

You may circle as a bee

to open a path to heart,
essence of sunshine.

You may offer butterflies
pollination of jasmine and rose.

You may emerge
from a cocoon of being

into butterfly just to
offer gratitude to bees,

subtle wings fluttering, prana
that hums into self,

nectar of being.

Maybe you will open

your heart and wait until
butterflies emerge

from soft cocoons.
Perhaps you will delight

in the flitting circles
that butterflies weave in air.

Offer what you can,
a blossom, fragrance of self,

a breeze rustle of your
soft rose petals; the heart

is not separate from this.

Perhaps you will carry

yourself as a bee
carries pollen so that

you can spin yourself
into honey. Collect

your smile, the light
in your eyes. Gather up

the body into sunshine
and soft flowers.

This is what you must
give in order to circle

as a bee always circles.

You can tend to yourself

in the garden of self.
You may then become

strength and humility,
a sunflower bowing.

Bees and butterflies will come
circling your lofty seed-head;

grace and gratitude,
a meeting of self

with self, a bee always
circling, subtle

vibration of prana.

You are a flower, a bee,

a butterfly who drinks
of yourself. Rooted

down you are both
insect and flower, nectar

and pollen. Who you are
does not matter as

much as this.
Where you circle,

there is always love;
you can always spin

yourself into being.

BREATH IN THE SHAPE OF A BEE

Breathing in the shape
of a bee
the body is
beating fast wings

to become
suspended in air.
You are hovering
over the poetry

of a rose bush
and sweet bloom
to inhale rose scent,
manna of self.

Inhale until
you become deep
and pliant like rose
heads opening.

There, in the shape
of a bee, your
wings are enough
for your body

to hover above
the velvet petals
of rose-manna
unfolding.

Breathe into
the manna-sweet
essence of being bee.
Breathing into

shape of rose
reveals to yourself
the shape
of your soul.

Into this, you
become substance
of wing beat,
heart, lungs, body.

Feed yourself
rose-manna until
you are heavy
with the dharma

of becoming.
Rose nectar makes
you directionless
and droopy. Inhale

into this
and you become
once again
the shape of a bee.

The shape of your
breath is the shape
of a bee strumming
ferociously delicate

wings. You eat
as much rose-manna
as the bee-body
can take in.

Heavy-bodied like this,
the only choice is to
breathe, bit by bit,
into the shape of a bee.

The shape of your
soul is bee-like.
Up, down, weaving
through air

as if searching for
rose-manna. Drink
in as much rose-scent
and nectar

as you can find
in order to carry
who you are
back to your hive.

In the shape of bee
you are breathing
in, out, up, down.
Wing beat,

wings beating
to hover in air;
deepen into rose
scent to see how

it leads you back
to self, to rose-manna,
exhale and inhale,
the dharma of being.

WATER BLESSING

Your eyes are as
deep and still
as a watery sinkhole

you come upon
after walking far
into woods.

Though you are one
with water already

you hesitate.
It is necessary, sometimes
to wait until

the breeze blows
water into ripples
so that you can see

where not to step, how not
to drown in yourself.

You may imagine
an aquifer
of your soul

pure and layered
deep, running
beneath strata

of dirt and clay,
shale and sandstone.

Earth is but
a blanket
covering you so that

you may surface
at the right time,
graceful as bubbling

of a spring, more
pure than a river.

The breeze
whispers before
it chants; amid

trees and boulders
the breeze leads
you to a place

where self surfaces
with ease.

Offer the natural spring
of self a water oblation,
even as you know

deep down
you are already
an aquifer,

surfacing in the woods
with gentle music.

You are already
complex matrices
of wood and stone.

Allow it and you can
build yourself
into a temple.

With you, the scent
of earthiness

is inescapable. Air,
moss, trees, rocks.
Beneath your breath

and body lays
a subtle brook. None
of these are separate.

You are already love,
whole and complete.

You are already
love, already water.
You are always

whispering
with the breeze
in a manner that heals.

Your voice whispers
a chant that thickens

the air into being.
There is no need
for sadness yet you offer

a kindness mantra,
a water blessing.
In your breath you transmit

the nature of love,
a mantra for being.

Amid trees you
can never lose
your way. Already

the breeze whispers
you into being,
into chant. Already

you are in leaves
that sound like oceans.

Perhaps the heart
moves you. Perhaps
water comes into your

eyes. Offer yourself
the moment becoming,
it is a water blessing:

May you be yourself.
May you be enough.

May you be as peaceful
as a quiet lake.
May you be as loved

as an aquifer surfacing
into a clear spring.
May you give yourself

to the breeze to chant.
Poetry may be

all that you offer
deep in the woods
for water to become.

You may sometimes
forget that you are
an aquifer, but

water will flow,
a water blessing.

WALK AMONG TREES

The heart is a map
of trees; spruce and oak,
birch and choke cherry.

Forest yourself
into this, follow a map
of willow and poplar,

maple and holly. See
how this leads you.

Leaves tell you
in their shapes
who you are, sawtooth

or smooth, oval
or ellipse. From shapes
of leaves in a forest

you can at last gather
who you become.

The way sunlight
sweeps through trees
is a map of the heart.

Sun settles into
nuanced patterns
in deep-seeded pines

so that you may see
the heart again.

In breeze, branches
reveal their green-gold
treasures. Open

your chest; the heart
sings the fullness
of trees gently swaying.

The breeze is a compass,
a direction to go.

Take yourself into woods
where trees are
a map of the heart.

Hawthorn and sweetgum,
elm and ash; walk
among trees with sunlight

and breeze stirring
a clear path.

BREATH INHALES

Scent of juniper
and pine,
oak tannin
and moss;

breeze stirring
across
the lake, shore
silt and stone;

shape of trees
and footprints
on a muddy
path.

Hint of red
sunrise
on sleeping
mountains, and

later,
pale deep
of sky brimming over
silver mountaintops until

clouds, steely
and swollen,
commence their
rain.

Breathe this in
without
exhale until
the heart

and sky
begin to clear
and the breath
takes in

again, sun,
moon,
stars,
universe.

STEP INTO A FOREST

Where there is a trail
through a forest
there is a possibility;

a forest offers itself
so that you can step
footfall into being.

A short walk or
miles, it does not
matter. You step

in and you are there.
The forest breathes.
You breathe.

A walk into woods
reveals the way
trees stretch to receive

light, rain, wind, moon.
A breeze can rustle trees
into soft whispers.

Wind can sway trees
into a chorus singing
as if waves of ocean.

You sing,
the forest sings.
Step in and you are there.

You are like a tree
in the sense that you
receive wind, rain, moon,

sun as a treasure. With you
there too is soft sway in
every intake, exhale.

Step into the forest;
a trail will lead you to
a church of your soul.

Go in. Where a trail
leads there is always
a possibility for being.

DEER CROSSING A RIVER

You are a like a deer
crossing a shallow
river, knowing

in water
there is love, in
the wild woods

there is no other
place as good
to shed

dirt from hoofs,
to cleanse
bottoms

of all you trampled.

What matters more
than forgiving
yourself for being

is being like a deer
crossing a river
with the sound

of water, heart-
beat, hoofs
splashing through

silence as if
cleansing your karmas
as much with love

as with water.

You are as a deer in
knowing the right
place to step

into love, to clear
all you have
trampled by being

unforgiving
of being, to wash
yourself into knowing

here is the right place
to step, to cleanse
karmas in a shallow

river's gentle flow.

SKY AS AN OCEAN

Maybe you swim
in high tide
among swells
of atmosphere.
There, clouds
crest as
whitecaps.

There, clouds
gather as
schools of fish.
This is a way
you love: to simply
be in sunshine
beneath a sky

so deep
it may as well
be an ocean.

You are part cloud
even here on
Earth's surface.
Condensation rises
and falls with
your breath.
Condense yourself

into clouds forming;
perhaps a way you
love is to
shapeshift
into your own
cloud body.
Maybe you even

collect yourself
into the shape
of a cloud-whale.

Perhaps you
are a cloud-whale
spouting ocean into
atmosphere. Dive
into the curve
and swell, dip
into atmospheric

lulls and vortexes
of self. Move
in your whale-
cloud-body and air
currents happen.
Swim and you see
this is how you

can love, there
with clouds forming,
in sky as an ocean.

SO BELOVED, BELOW

Here is your spirit

opening to see
how light coming

through trees is an
act of devotion: gold-green,

dappling; light on
the forest floor. Om Tare

Tuttare Ture Swaha.

Open and you will

spill seeds of the sun
onto yourself.

Let water into
your eyes

so that you can grow
into spindles

of maple and beech.

Here in the forest

is a place to be
quiet and hear

how the breeze opens
your voice beneath

leaf-lush trees to sing
Om Tare Tuttare

Ture Swaha.

Light coming

through treetops
is an act of compassion;

open your heart
to see star-flowers

grow in soft maple-beech
places where stippling

sunlight comes through.

Stand still

in your maple-ness.
Sunlight will

always streak
with devotion through

your gold-green
soft leaves, Om Tare

Tuttare Ture Swaha.

Above, below,

stand firm
in your beech-ness;

in trees green-
gold cascades into

the heart of the woods;
in soft sunlight

hearts converge.

Om Tare

Tuttare Ture
Swaha. Stars above

and below, bright petals
flame into

soft stars and nebulae;
yellow, blue,

soft burnished gold.

Here is your spirit

becoming soft, sweet
like the petals

of tiny star-flowers
growing beneath maples

and beech; sunlight
spotting where lokas

converge from above, below.

Open your heart

like flower heads
bursting into tiny

nebulae so beloved,
below; lokas converge

in your heart, spirit:
Om Tare

Tuttare Ture Swaha.

TREE-SOUL

Rise, fall, return to yourself
as a breeze stirring leaves
into music, earth into mountains.

Somewhere above the tops
of trees you are the taste
of ozone. Beneath this

you become deep
and cloudless, atmosphere.
You move in a subtle

circle through cold to warm;
oxygen, carbon dioxide,
tree-soul, human.

You contain mountains
in your heart. When you breathe
mountains release themselves

to you. You are the cold
of snowmelt turning soft streams
into rivers that rush

into lowland lakes. You are flowing
of water into the deep
of earth, unsurfacing

into aquifers. Only this is enough
for your tree-self soul,
for being human.

You are the strength of tree-
roots extending into depth
of earth, wanting to drink

cool water from the aquifer
of your own heart. There in
the deep you know who

you are, tree-soul, human.
Roots grow, the trunk
of the body stretches you

into sky, branches extending.
This may be how you become
like light from the sun.

You are the dappling greens
and yellows of foliage
swaying in sunlight.

How you become your
tree-soul self, humanness,
in the movement

of branches stretching outward,
skyward, is all that matters.
You become the subtleness

of oak scent and tannin.
Beneath this you are still
an aquifer, always earthing.

Deepening into woods
you become the same
as the scent of soft moss,

the feel of cool air beneath
canopies of green,
the sound of small things

in the underbrush stirring.
When you are all this
you are also softer than

a stream flowing over
worn rocks, waterflows, the cycling
of tree-self soul, human, becoming.

TIGER LILY

Drink in, drink in
cool water from
your stream of being.

Wild at heart, unfold
the beauty
of your own bloom.

Strong in the sun, a
tiger lily unbound,
Om Suryaya
Namaha, Om.

Unfold forgiveness
as a tiger lily
unfurls its breadth.

You can be as soft
as petals that stretch
and beam;

you can be as strong
as the sturdy stalk
growing wild near a brook.

Soft as a mantra
that comes steadily
into your heart,

let go, let go now
of names and hurts,
of abandonment.

There is no place
in the self that requires
a residence of pain.

Om Suryaya Namaha,
Om. Take down
the tufted edges

of your hurts.
In summer you become.
In sunlight you are grace.

Take down, take down
winter, spring.
The heart requires this.

Stand in water.
Stand in a stream
in the wild woods.

The heart expects
no less than this.
Listen; soft as mantra

water sings. Sink
your roots in wherever
water flows, let go.

Open your gorgeous
flower head.
Unfurl your petals

to become a tiger
lily whose beauty
quells any

doubt. This is who
you are; who you
have always been.

Tiger in the depth
of sun, lily in light.
Open and receive,

open and give.
Stand in a stream
of water and admit

this is who you have
become. Om Suryaya
Namaha, Om.

ALWAYS

Always, you say
you want to be
a meteor

falling into
streaks of fire
in night sky.

When you fall
to earth you
become ash.

When you fall
from night you
become day.

In the ashen sky
before dawn
you always see

it is still possible
to find yourself
in a morning star.

In morning you are
always listening for
birds to begin

their songs of day.
You always say
you want to have

wings to fly above
treetops and into
mountains. When

you fly you will
be like Icarus
moving towards

the sun with waxy
wings. You may fall
but in falling

you will always see
how softly trees extend
to sky to catch you.

Brief descriptions of mantra-related words appearing in this book:

Dharma – right way of living, one's life purpose

Karma - cause and effect; the sum of a person's actions carried into or created
    in this lifetime

Loka – heavenly and earthly realms of existence

Manna – spiritual nourishment

Marichaye – sunlight corresponding to dawn and dusk

Prana – lifeforce energy

Om – that which is all encompassing, the sound of the universe

Om Marichaye, Om Marichaye Namaha, Om Marichaye Om – variations
    meaning salutations to the pure light of the Sun at dawn/dusk

Om Suryaya Namaha – salutations to the Sun god/Sun

Om Tare Tuttare Ture Swaha – salutations to goddess Tara, who has multiple
    manifestations. In the context of this poem, she is Tara, goddess of nature
    or forest goddess.

ABOUT THE AUTHOR

Audrey Tanner, Ed.D., is a poet and healer dedicated to the art of self-restoration. As a Reiki Master in the Usui lineage and a certified teacher of yoga and meditation, her writing is an extension of her spiritual practice—a bridge between the physical landscape and the inner soul.

With a doctorate in higher education leadership and over 30 years of university experience, Audrey blends a grounded, scholarly perspective with a deep mastery of Sanskrit mantra and mindfulness. A graduate of the UCLA Extension fiction writing program, she now explores the "quiet magic" of the world through poetry and creative nonfiction.

audreytannerwrites.com

MORE BY AUDREY TANNER

RIVER DREAM: Peaceful poems for meditation, self-reflection, daydreaming, and dreams. Nature as a presence that guides the journey into the depth of self.

KARMAS, LIKE HEARTS: A poetry chapbook. Poems about an experience of loss, grief, and recovery that guide the reader with grace from loss to light.

SOFT ARRIVALS: Poems from Madeira Island that emerge through Maderia's natural beauty and historic culture. An invitation to the reader to slow down, breathe, and find their way home to themselves.

SLOW MOVING CLOUDS: Poems from Madeira Island that invite the reader into a peaceful experience of awarenesses, imagination, and self-renewal within an atmospheric quietness born of the island's natural beauty.